MYSTICAL BUDDHISM

IN CONNEXION WITH

THE YOGA PHILOSOPHY

OF

THE HINDUS.

BY

SIR MONIER MONIER-WILLIAMS, K.C.I.E.
D.C.L. LL.D.
Boden Professor of Sanskrit in the University of Oxford.

ANNUAL ADDRESS READ BEFORE THE VICTORIA INSTITUTE, OR
PHILOSOPHICAL SOCIETY OF GREAT BRITAIN.
4 JUNE, 1888.

Copyright © 2018 Read Books Ltd.
This book is copyright and may not be
reproduced or copied in any way without
the express permission of the publisher in writing

British Library Cataloguing-in-Publication Data
A catalogue record for this book is available from
the British Library

Yoga

'Yoga' is the physical, mental and spiritual practices or disciplines which originated in ancient India, with a view to 'attain a state of permanent peace.' The term yoga can be derived from either of two roots, *yujir yoga* (to yoke) or *yuj samādhau* (to concentrate). The ultimate goal of Yoga is *moksha* (liberation), though the exact definition of what form this takes depends on the philosophical or theological system with which it is conjugated. The *Yoga Sūtras of Patañjali* (one of the oldest and most renowned yoga texts) defines yoga as 'the stilling of the changing states of the mind', yet alternatively, yoga has been popularly defined as 'union with the divine.' Various traditions of yoga are found in the ancient religions of Hinduism, Buddhism and Jainism. It is also an important part of Vajrayana and Tibetan Buddhist philosophy.

The origins of yoga are a matter of debate. It may have pre-Vedic origins, as several seals, discovered at Indus Valley Civilisation sites depict figures in positions resembling a common yoga or meditation pose. Ascetic practices, concentration and bodily postures used by Vedic priests (mainly to conduct the ritual of fire sacrifice) may have been precursors to yoga. Nonetheless, these pre–philosophical speculations and diverse ascetic practices of first millennium BCE were systematized into a formal philosophy by the *Yoga Sutras of Patanjali*. Patanjali was also the founder of the yoga school of philosophy. By the turn of the first millennium, hatha yoga had emerged from tantra. This latter practice, 'Tantrism' is a mode of yoga supposed to alter the relation of its practitioners to the ordinary social, religious, and logical reality in which they live. Through Tantric practice, an individual perceives reality as 'maya'; illusion, and achieves liberation from it. Both Tantra and more common forms of yoga offer paths that relieve a person from worldly dependence.

Where many yogic practices rely on progressive restriction of inputs from outside; Tantra relies on transmutation of all external inputs so that one is no longer dependent on them, but can take them or leave them at will. This particular path to salvation, among the several offered by Hinduism, links Tantrism to those practices of Indian religions, such as meditation, and social renunciation, which are based on temporary or permanent withdrawal from social relationships and modes. It, along with its many modern variations, is the style that many people associate with the word *yoga* today. 'Hatha' in specific has incredibly long roots however, with the earliest references found in Buddhist works dating from the eighth century. The basic tenets of Hatha yoga were formulated by Shaiva ascetics Matsyendranath and Gorakshanath c. 900 CE. Hatha yoga synthesizes elements of Patanjali's *Yoga Sutras* with posture and breathing exercises – focusing on the purification of the physical body, which will then lead to the purification of the mind (ha) and *prana,* or vital energy (tha). It utilises full body postures (now widely exploited), a development on the original seated asanas. Body, mind and meditation are all closely linked.

The first Hindu teacher to actively advocate and disseminate aspects of yoga to a western audience, Swami Vivekananda, toured Europe and the United States in the 1890s. The reception Swami Vivekananda received built on the active interest of intellectuals, in particular the New England Transcendentalists, among them R. W. Emerson (1803-1882), who drew on German Romanticism and the interest of philosophers and scholars like G. F. W. Hegel (1770-1831), the Schlegel brothers, A. Schopenhauer (1788-1860) and others who had (to varying degrees) interests in Indian culture. Following on from Swami Vivekananda's great success, many more Gurus from India travelled to the west, introducing yogic techniques. As a result of this, from the 1890s onwards, yoga has become popular as an all-encompassing system of physical exercise across the world.

A second 'yoga boom' followed in the 1980s, as Dean Ornish, a follower of Swami Satchidananda, connected yoga to heart health, legitimizing yoga as a purely physical system of health exercises. This brought it outside of counter-culture or esotericism circles, and unconnected to any religious denomination; the modern form of hatha which many practice today. In a national survey, long-term yoga practitioners in the United States reported musculo–skeletal and mental health improvements, and there is evidence to suggest that regular yoga practice increases brain GABA levels and improves mood and anxiety more than other similar exercises. The three main focuses of Hatha yoga (exercise, breathing, and meditation) make it especially beneficial to those suffering from heart disease. To remain with the United States (a country with the highest percentage of yoga practitioners in the western-world), since 2001, the popularity of yoga has risen constantly. The number of people who practiced some form of yoga has grown from 4 million (in 2001) to 20 million (in 2011). It is amazing, that although in altered form – yoga, from such ancient traditions, is still so relevant and so cherished by people across the globe. Namaste.

MYSTICAL BUDDHISM IN CONNEXION WITH THE YOGA PHILOSOPHY OF THE HINDUS. By Sir Monier Monier-Williams, K.C.I.E., D.C.L., LL.D., Ph.D., Boden Professor of Sanskrit in the University of Oxford.*

THE first idea implied by Buddhism is intellectual enlightenment. But Buddhism has its own theory of enlightenment—its own idea of true knowledge, which it calls Bodhi, not Veda. By true knowledge it means knowledge acquired by man through his own intellectual faculties and through his own inner consciousness, instincts, and intuitions, unaided by any external or supernatural revelation of any kind.

But it is important to observe that Buddhism, in the carrying out of its own theory of entire self-dependence in the search after truth, was compelled to be somewhat inconsistent with itself. It enjoined self-conquest, self-restraint, self-concentration and separation from the world for the attainment of perfect knowledge and for the accomplishment of its own *summum bonum*—the bliss of Nirvāna—the bliss of deliver-

---

* In this paper some of the diacritical marks, required for the accurate representation of Oriental words in the Roman character, have been omitted.

ance from the fires of passion and the flames of concupiscence. Yet it encouraged association and combination for mutual help. It established a universal brotherhood of celibate monks, open to persons of all castes and ranks, to rich and poor, learned and unlearned alike—a community of men which might, in theory, be co-extensive with the whole world—all bound together by the common aim of self-conquest, all animated by the wish to aid each other in the battle with carnal desires, all penetrated by a desire to follow the example of the Buddha, and be guided by the doctrine or law which he promulgated.

Cœnobitic monasticism in fact became an essential part of true Buddhism and a necessary instrument for its propagation.

In all this the Buddha showed himself to be eminently practical in his methods and profoundly wise in his generation. Evidently, too, he was wise in abstaining at first from all mystical teaching. Originally Buddhism set its face against all solitary asceticism and secret efforts to attain sublime heights of knowledge. It had no occult, no esoteric system of doctrine which it withheld from ordinary men.

Nor did true Buddhism at first concern itself with any form of philosophical or metaphysical teaching, which it did not consider helpful for the attainment of the only kind of true knowledge worth striving for—the knowledge of the origin of suffering and its remedy—the knowledge that suffering and pain arise from indulging lusts, and that life is inseparable from suffering, and is an evil to be got rid of by suppressing self and extinguishing desires.

In the *Mahā-parinibbāna-sutta* (Rhys Davids, 11–32) is recorded one of the Buddha's remarks shortly before his decease.

"What, O Ananda, does the Order desire of me? I have taught the law (desito dhammo) without making any distinction between esoteric and exoteric doctrine (anantaram abahiram karitvā). In the matter of the law, the Tathāgata (*i.e.*, the Buddha) has never had the closed fist of a teacher (ācariya-mutthi)—that is of a teacher who withholds some doctrines and communicates others."

Nevertheless, admitting, as we must, that early Buddhism had no mysteries reserved for a privileged circle, we must not shut our eyes to the fact that the great importance attached to abstract meditation in the Buddhist system could not fail in the end to encourage the growth of mystical ideas.

Furthermore, it is undeniable that such ideas were, in some countries, carried to the most extravagant extremes. Efforts to induce a trance-like or hypnotic condition, by abstracting the thoughts from all bodily influences, by recitation of mystical sentences and by superstitious devices for the acquisition of supernatural faculties, were placed above good works and all the duties of the moral code.

We might point, too, to the strange doctrine which arose in Nepal and Tibet—the doctrine of the Dhyāni-Buddhas (or Buddhas of Meditation)—certain abstract essences existing in the formless worlds of thought, who were held to be ethereal and eternal representatives of the transitory earthly Buddhas.

Our present concern, however, is rather with the growth and development of mystical Buddhism in India itself, through its connexion with the system called Yoga and Yogācāra.

The close relationship of Buddhism to that system is well known. The various practices included under the name Yoga did not owe their origin to Buddhism. They were prevalent in India before Gautama Buddha's time; and one of the most generally accepted facts in his biography is that, after abandoning his home and worldly associations, he resorted to certain Brāhman ascetics, who were practising Yoga.

What then was the object which these ascetics had in view?

The word Yoga literally means "union" (as derived from the Sanskrit root "yuj," to join), and the proper aim of every man who practised Yoga was the mystic union (or rather re-union) of his own spirit with the one eternal Soul or Spirit of the Universe, and the acquisition of divine knowledge through that union.

It may be taken for granted that this was the Buddha's first aim when he addressed himself to Yoga in the fifth century B.C., and even to this hour, earnest men in India resort to this system with the same object.

In the *Indian Magazine* for July, 1887 (as well as in my *Brāhmanism and Hindūism**) is a short biography of a quite recent religious reformer named Svāmī Dayānanda Sarasvatī, whose acquaintance I made at Bombay in 1876 and 1877, and who only died in 1883. The story of his life reads almost like a repetition of the life of Buddha, though his teaching aimed at restoring the supposed monotheistic doctrine of the Veda.

It is recorded that his father, desiring to initiate him into the mysteries of Saivism, took him to a shrine dedicated to the god Siva; but the sight of some mice stealing the consecrated offerings and of some rats playing on the heads of the idol led him to disbelieve in Siva-worship as a means of union with the Supreme Being. Longing, however, for such union

---

* Published by John Murray, Albemarle Street (see p. 529).

and for emancipation from the burden of repeated births, he resolved to renounce marriage and abandon the world. Accordingly, at the age of twenty-two, he clandestinely quitted his home, the darkness of evening covering his flight. Taking a secret path, he travelled thirty miles during the night. Next day he was pursued by his father, who tried to force him to return, but in vain. After travelling farther and farther from his native province, he took a vow to devote himself to the investigation of truth. Then he wandered for many years all over India, trying to gain knowledge from sages and philosophers, but without any satisfactory result, till finally he settled at Ahmedabad. There, having mastered the higher Yoga system, he became the leader of a new sect called the Ārya-Samāj.

And here we may observe that the expression "higher Yoga" implies that another form of that system was introduced. In point of fact, the Yoga system grew, and became twofold—that is, it came in the end to have two objects.

The earlier was the higher Yoga. It aimed only at union with the Spirit of the Universe. The more developed system aimed at something more. It sought to acquire miraculous powers by bringing the body under control of the will, and by completely abstracting the soul from body and mind, and isolating it in its own essence. This condition is called Kaivalya.

In the fifth century B.C., when Gautama Buddha began his career, the later and lower form of Yoga seems to have been little known. Practically, in those days earnest and devout men craved only for union with the Supreme Being, and absorption into his essence. Many methods of effecting such union and absorption were contrived. And these may be classed under two chief heads—bodily mortification (tapas) and abstract meditation (dhyāna).

By either one of these two chief means, the devotee was supposed to be able to get rid of all bodily fetters—to be able to bring his bodily organs into such subjection to the spiritual that he became unconscious of possessing any body at all. It was in this way that his spirit became fit for blending with the Supreme Spirit.

We learn from the *Lalita-vistara* that various forms of bodily torture, self-maceration, and austerity were common in Gautama's time.

Some devotees, we read, seated themselves in one spot and kept perpetual silence, with their legs bent under them. Some ate only once a day or once on alternate days, or at intervals of four, six, or fourteen days. Some slept in wet clothes or on ashes, gravel, stones, boards, thorny grass, or spikes, or with the face downwards. Some went naked, making no distinction between fit or unfit places. Some smeared themselves with ashes, cinders, dust, or clay. Some inhaled smoke and fire. Some gazed at the sun, or sat surrounded by five fires, or rested on one foot, or kept one arm perpetually uplifted, or moved about on their knees instead of on their feet, or baked themselves on hot stones, or entered water, or suspended themselves in the air.

Then, again, a method of fasting called very painful (atikricchra), described by Manu (xi. 213), was often practised. It consisted in eating only a single mouthful every day for nine days and then abstaining from all food for the three following days.

Another method, called the lunar fast (vi. 20, xi. 216), consisted in beginning with fifteen mouthfuls at full moon, and reducing the quantity by one mouthful till new moon, and then increasing it again in the same way till full moon.

Passages without number might be quoted from ancient literature to prove that similar practices were resorted to throughout India with the object of bringing the body into subjection to the spirit. And these practices have continued up to the present day.

A Muhammadan traveller, whose narrative is quoted by Mr. Mill (*British India*, I. 355), once saw a man standing motionless with his face towards the sun.

The same traveller, having occasion to revisit the same spot sixteen years afterwards, found the very same man in the very same attitude. He had gazed on the sun's disk till all sense of external vision was extinguished.

A Yogī was seen not very long ago (Mill's *India*, I. 353) seated between four fires on a quadrangular stage. He stood on one leg gazing at the sun, while these fires were lighted at the four corners. Then placing himself upright on his head, with his feet elevated in the air, he remained for three hours in that position. He then seated himself cross-legged, and continued bearing the raging heat of the sun above his head and the fires which surrounded him till the end of the day, occasionally adding combustibles with his own hands to increase the flames.

I, myself, in the course of my travels, encountered Yogīs who had kept their arms uplifted for years, or had wandered about from one place of pilgrimage to another under a perpetual vow of silence, or had no place to lie upon but a bed of spikes.

As to fasting, the idea that attenuation of the body by abstinence from food, facilitates union of the human soul with the divine, or at any rate promotes a keener insight into spiritual things, is doubtless as common in Europe as in Asia; but the most austere observer of Lent in European countries would be hopelessly outdone by devotees whose extraordinary powers of abstinence may be witnessed in every part of India.

If we now turn to the second great method of attaining mystic union with the Divine Essence, namely, by profound abstract thought, we may observe that it, too, was everywhere prevalent in Buddha's time.

Indeed, one of the names given by Indian philosophers to the One Universal Spirit is Cit, "Thought." By that name of course, is meant pure abstract thought, or the faculty of thought separated from every concrete object. Hence, in its highest state the eternal infinite Spirit, by its very nature, thinks of nothing. It is the simple thought faculty, wholly unconnected with any object, about which it thinks. In point of fact, the moment it begins to exercise this faculty, it necessarily abandons for a time its condition of absolute oneness, abstraction and isolation, to associate itself with something inferior, which is not itself.

It follows, therefore, that intense concentration of the mind on the One Universal Spirit amounts to fixing the thought on a mere abstract Essence, which reciprocates no thought in return, and is not conscious of being thought about by its worshipper.

In harmony with this theory, we find that the definition of Yoga, in the second aphorism of the Yoga-sūtra, is, "the suppression (nirodha) of the functions or modifications (vritti) of the thinking principle (citta)." So that, in reality, the union of the human mind with the infinite Principle of thought amounts to such complete mental absorption, that thought itself becomes lost in pure thought.

In the *Sakuntalā* (vii. 175) there is a description of an ascetic engaged in this form of Yoga, whose condition of fixed meditation and immovable impassiveness had lasted so long that ants had thrown up a mound as high as his waist, and birds had built their nests in the long clotted tresses of his tangled hair.

Not very dissimilar phenomena may be witnessed even in the present day. I, myself, not many years ago, saw at Allahabad a devotee who had maintained a sitting, contemplative posture with his feet folded under his body, in one place near the fort for twenty years.

During the Mutiny cannon thundered over his head, and bullets hissed all around him, but nothing apparently disturbed his attitude of profound meditation.

It is clear, then, from all we have stated, that, supposing Gautama to have made up his mind to renounce the world and devote himself to a religious life, his adoption of a course of Yoga was a most ordinary proceeding.

In the first instance, as we have seen, he tested the value of painful self-mortification by a long sexennial fast. Then, after discovering the uselessness of mere bodily austerities, he took food naturally, and adopting the second method, applied himself to profound abstract meditation.

A large number of the images of Buddha represent him sitting on a raised seat, with his legs folded under his body, and his eyes half-closed, in this condition of abstraction (samādhi)—sometimes called Yoga-nidrā; that is, a trance-like state, compared to profound sleep, or a kind of hypnotism.

According to the account given in the *Mahā-vagga* (i. 1), he seated himself in this way under four trees in succession, remaining absorbed in thought for seven days and nights under each tree, till he was, so to speak, re-born as Buddha "the Enlightened." Till then he had no right to that title.

And those four successive seats probably symbolised the four recognised stages of meditation* (dhyāna) rising one above the other, till thought itself was converted into non-thought.

We know, too, that the Buddha went through still higher progressive stages of meditation at the moment of his death or final decease (Pari-nirvāna), thus described in the *Mahā-parinibbāna sutta* (vi. 11):

"Then the Venerable One entered into the first stage of meditation (pathamajjhānam); and rising out of the first stage, he passed into the second; and rising out of the second, he passed into the third; and rising out of the third, he passed into the fourth; and rising out of the fourth stage, he attained the conception of the infinity of space (ākāsānan-cāyatanam); and rising out of the conception of the infinity of space, he attained the conception of the infinity of intelligence (or second Arūpa-brahma-loka). And rising out of the idea of the infinity of intelligence, he attained the conception of absolute nonentity (ākiñcaññāyatanam); and rising out of the idea of nonentity, he entered the region where there is neither consciousness nor unconsciousness; and rising out of that region, he entered the state in which all sensation and all perception of ideas had wholly ceased."

This strange passage shows that even four progressive

---

* I give this as a theory of my own. M. Senart considers that the sun's progress is symbolised. I am no believer in the sun theory as applicable to this point.

stages of abstraction did not satisfy the requirements of later Buddhism in regard to the intense sublimation of the thinking faculty needed for the complete effacement of all sense of individuality. Higher and higher altitudes had to be reached, insomuch that the fourth stage of abstract meditation is sometimes divided and sub-divided into what are called eight vimokhas and eight samāpattis—all of them forms and stages of ecstatic meditation.*

A general name, however, for all the higher trance-like states is *Samādhi*, and by the practice of Samādhi the six transcendent faculties (Abhiññā) might ultimately be obtained, viz., the inner ear, or power of hearing words and sounds however distant (clair-audience, as it might be called), the inner eye or power of seeing all that happens in every part of the world (clair-voyance), knowledge of the thoughts of others, recollection of former existences, the knowledge of the mode of destroying the corrupting influences of passion, and, finally, the supernatural powers called Iddhi, to be subsequently explained.

But to return to the Buddha's first course of meditation at the time when he first attained Buddhahood. This happened during one particular night, which was followed by the birthday of Buddhism.

And what was the first grand outcome of that first profound mental abstraction? One legend relates that in the first watch of the night all his previous existences flashed across his mind; in the second he understood all present states of being; in the third he traced out the chain of causes and effects, and at the dawn of day he knew all things.

According to another legend, there was an actual outburst of the divine light before hidden within him.

We read in the *Lalita-vistara* (chap. i.) that at the supreme moment of his intellectual illumination brilliant flames of light issued from the crown of his head, through the interstices of his cropped hair. These rays are sometimes represented in his images, emerging from his skull in a form resembling the five fingers of an extended hand.

Mark, however, that it is never stated that Gautama ever attained to the highest result of the true Yoga of Indian philosophy—union with the Supreme Spirit. On the contrary, his self-enlightenment led to entire disbelief in the separate existence of any eternal, infinite Spirit at all—any Spirit, in fact, with which a spirit existing in his own body could blend, or into which it could be absorbed.

---

* These are described in Childers's *Pāli Dictionary*, s.v.

If the Buddha was not a materialist, in the sense of believing in the eternal existence of material atoms, neither could he in any sense be called a "spiritualist," or "spiritist."

With him Creation did not proceed from an Omnipotent Spirit evolving phenomena out of itself by the exercise of almighty will, nor from an eternal self-existing, self-evolving germ of any kind. As to the existence of any spiritual substance in the Universe which was not matter and was imperceptible by the senses, it could not be proved.

Nor did he believe in the eternal existence of an invisible, intangible, human self or Ego, commonly called Soul, as distinct from a material body. In this he differed widely from the Yoga. The only eternity of early Buddhism was in an eternity of "becoming," not of "being"—an eternity of universes, all succeeding each other, and all lapsing into nothingness.

In short, the Buddha's enlightenment consisted, first, in the discovery of the origin and remedy of suffering, and, next, in the knowledge of the existence of an eternal Force—a force generated by what in Sanskrit is called Karman, " Act." Who, or what, started the first act the Buddha never pretended to be able to explain. He confessed himself in regard to this point a downright Agnostic.

All he affirmed was that every man was created by the force of his own acts in former bodies, combined with a force generated by intense attachment to existence (upādāna). The Buddha himself was so created, and had been created and re-created through countless bodily forms; but he had no spirit or soul existing separately between the intervals of each creation. By his protracted meditation he attained to no higher knowledge than this, and although he himself rose to loftier heights of knowledge than any other man of his day, he never aspired to other than the extraordinary faculties which were within the reach of any human being capable of rising to the same sublime abstraction of mind.

He was even careful to lay down a precept that the acquisition of transcendent human faculties was restricted to the perfected saints called Arhats; and so important did he consider it to guard such faculties from being claimed by mere impostors, that one of the four prohibitions communicated to all monks on first admission to his monastic Order was that they were not to pretend to such powers.

Nor is there any proof that even Arhats in Gautama's time were allowed to claim the power of working physical miracles.

By degrees, no doubt, powers of this kind were ascribed to them as well as to the Buddha. Even in the Vinaya, one of the oldest portions of the *Tripitaka*, we find it stated that Gautama Buddha gained adherents by performing three thousand five hundred supernatural wonders (in Pāli pātihāriya). These were thought to be evidences of his mission as a great teacher and saviour of mankind; but the part of the narrative recording these, although very ancient, is probably a legendary addition of later date. It is interesting, however, to trace in other portions of the first literature, the development of the doctrine that Buddhahood meant first transcendent knowledge, and then supernatural faculties, and finally miraculous powers.

In the *Akkanheyya Sutta* (said to be written in the fourth century B.C.) occurs this remarkable passage, translated by Professor Rhys Davids (p. 214):—

"If a Monk should desire through the destruction of the corrupting influences (āsavas), by himself, and even in this very world, to know and realise and attain to Arhatship, to emancipation of heart, and emancipation of mind, let him devote himself to that quietude of heart which springs from within, let him not drive back the ecstasy of contemplation, let him look through things, let him be much alone.

"If a Monk should desire to hear with clear and heavenly ear, surpassing that of men, sounds both human and celestial, whether far or near; if he should desire to comprehend by his own heart the hearts of other beings and of other men; if he should desire to call to mind his various temporary states in the past, such as one, two, three, four, five, ten, twenty, a hundred, a thousand, a hundred thousand births, or his births in many an age and æon of destruction and renovation, let him devote himself to that quietude which springs from within."

Then, in the *Mahā-parinibbāna-sutta* (i. 33) occurs the following:—

"At that time the Blessed One—as instantaneously as a strong man would stretch forth his arm, or draw it back again when he had stretched it forth—vanished from this side of the river, and stood on the further bank with the company of the brethren."

And, again, the following:—

"I call to mind, Ānanda, how when I used to enter into an assembly of many hundred nobles, before I had seated myself there, or talked to them, or started a conversation with them, I used to become in colour like unto their colour, and in voice like unto their voice. Then, with religious discourse, I used to instruct, incite, and quicken them, and fill them with gladness. But they knew me not when I spoke, and would say, 'Who may this be who thus speaks? a man or a god?' Then, having instructed, incited, quickened and gladdened them with religious discourse, I would vanish away. But they knew me not even when I vanished away; and would say, 'Who may this be who has thus vanished away? a man, or a god?'" (Mahā-parinibbāna-sutta, iii. 22.)

Such passages in the early literature afford an interesting examplification of the growth of supernatural and mystical ideas, and account for the ultimate association of the Northern Buddhistic system, with Saivism, demonology, magic, and various spiritual phenomena connected with what has been called "Esoteric Buddhism."

These ideas, however, originated in India, and we may now proceed to trace their development in the later *Yoga* or "aphorisms of the Yoga philosophy," composed by Patanjali, to which I have already referred.

In that work eight requisites of Yoga are enumerated (ii. 29); namely 1, abstaining from five evil acts (yama); 2, performing five positive duties (niyama); 3, settling the limbs in certain postures (āsana); 4, regulating and suppressing the breath (prānāyāma); 5, withdrawing the senses from their objects (pratyāhāra); 6, fixing the thinking faculty (dhāranā); 7, internal self-contemplation (dhyāna); 8, trance-like self-concentration (samādhi).

These eight are indispensable requisites for the gaining of Patanjali's *summum bonum*—the complete abstraction or isolation (kaivalya) of the soul in its own essence and for the acquirement of supernatural faculties.

Taking now these eight requisites of Yoga in order, we may observe, with regard to the first, that the five evil acts to be avoided correspond to the five commandments in Buddhism, viz., "kill not," "steal not," "commit no impurity," "lie not." The fifth alone, "abstain from all worldly enjoyments," is different, the Buddhist fifth prohibition being "drink no strong drink."

With regard to the second requisite, the five positive duties are—self-purification, both external and internal (both called sauca); the practice of contentment (santosha); bodily mortification (tapas); muttering of prayers, or repetition of mystical syllables (svādhyāya, or japa), and contemplation of the Supreme Being.

The various processes of bodily mortification and austerities have been already described.

As to the muttering of prayers, the repetition of mystic syllables such as Om (a symbol for the Triad of Gods), or of any favourite deity's name, is held among Hindūs to be highly efficacious.* In a similar manner among Northern Buddhists the six-syllabled sentence: "Om mani padme hūm"—"Reverence to the jewel in the lotus. Amen"—is used as a charm against the sixfold course of transmigration. The Jewel may mean Avalokitesvara, the patron saint of Tibet, fabled to have sprung from a lotus, or it may contain a *double-entendre*—an occult allusion to the Sānkhya Purusha and Prakriti, or to the Linga and Yoni of Saivism, as symbolising the generative force of Nature. No other prayer-formula in the world is repeated so often.

Other mystical syllables (such as sam, yam, ram, lam) are supposed to contain some occult virtue.

The third requisite—posture—would appear to us a somewhat trivial aid to the union of the human spirit with the divine; but with Hindūs it is an important auxiliary, fraught with great benefit to the Yogī.

The alleged reason is that certain sitting postures (āsana) and cramping of the lower limbs are peculiarly efficacious in producing bodily quietude and preventing restlessness. Some of the postures have curious names, for example:— Padmāsana, "the lotus posture"; vīrāsana, "the heroic posture"; sinhāsana, "the lion posture"; kūrmāsana, "the tortoise posture"; kukkutāsana, "the cock posture"; dhanur-āsana, "bow posture"; mayūrāsana, "peacock posture." In the first the right foot is placed on the left thigh, and the left on the right thigh.

In short, the idea is that compression of the lower limbs, in such a way as to prevent the possibility of the slightest movement, is most important as a preparation for complete abstraction of soul.

Then, as another aid, particular twistings (called mudrā) of the upper limbs—of the arms, hands, and fingers—are enjoined.

In Europe violent movements of the limbs are practised by devotees with the view of uniting the human spirit with the Divine. Those who have seen the whirling and "howling" dervishes of Cairo can testify to this. The fainting fits which result from their violent exertions, inspirations, expirations, and utterances of the name of God are believed to be ecstatic states in which such union is effected.

The fourth requisite—regulation and suppression of the breath—is perhaps the one of all the eight which it is most difficult for Europeans to understand or appreciate; yet with Hindūs it is all-important (being called Hatha-vidyā). Nor are the ideas connected with it wholly unknown in Europe.

---

* See my *Brāhmanism and Hindūism* (John Murray), p. 105.

According to Swedenborg,* thought commences and corresponds with respiration:—

"When a man thinks quickly his breath vibrates with rapid alternations; when the tempest of anger shakes his mind his breath is tumultuous; when his soul is deep and tranquil, so is his respiration." And he adds: "It is strange that this correspondence between the states of the brain or mind and the lungs has not been admitted in science."

The Hindū belief certainly is that deep inspirations of breath assist in concentrating and abstracting the thoughts and preventing external impressions. But, more than this, five sorts of air are supposed to permeate the human body and play an important part in its vitality. The Hatha-dīpikā says: "As long as the air remains in the body, so long life remains. Death is the exit of the breath. Hence the air should be retained in the body."

In regulating the breath, the air must first be drawn up through one nostril (the other being closed with the finger), retained in the lungs, and then expelled through the other nostril. This exercise must be practised alternately with the right and left nostril. Next, the breath must be drawn forcibly up through both nostrils, and the air imprisoned for as long a time as possible in the lungs. Thence it must be forced by an effort of will towards the internal organs of the body, or made to mount to the centre of the brain.

The Hindūs, however, do not identify the breath with the soul. They believe that a crevice or suture called the Brahma-randhram at the top of the skull serves as an outlet for the escape of the soul at death. A Hindū Yogī's skull is sometimes split at death by striking it with a sacred shell. The idea is to facilitate the exit of the soul. It is said that in Tibet the hair is torn out of the top of the head, with the same object.

In the case of a wicked man the soul is supposed to escape through one of the lower openings of the body.

The imprisonment of the breath in the body by taking in more air than is necessary for respiration, is the most important of the breath exercises. It is said that Hindū ascetics, by constant practice, are able by this means to sustain life under water, or to be buried alive for long periods of time. Such feats of endurance would be wholly impracticable in the case of Europeans. It seems, however, open to question, whether or not it may not be possible for human beings of particular constitutions to practise a kind of

---

* Quoted in Colonel Olcott's *Yoga Philosophy*, p. 282.

hibernation like that of animals, by some method of suspending temporarily the organic functions. A certain Colonel Townsend is said to have succeeded in doing so.

A well-known instance of suspended animation occurred in the Punjāb in 1837. A certain Yogī was there, by his own request, buried alive in a vault for forty days in the presence of Ruṇjit Singh and Sir Claude Wade; his eyes, ears, and every orifice of his body having been first stopped with plugs of wax. Dr. McGregor, the then residency surgeon, also watched the case. Every precaution was taken to prevent deception. English officials saw the man buried, as well as exhumed, and a perpetual guard over the vault was kept night and day by order of Runjit Singh himself. At the end of forty days the disinterment took place. The body was dried up like a stick, and the tongue, which had been turned back into the throat, had become like a piece of horn. Those who exhumed him followed his previously-given directions for the restoration of animation, and the Yogī told them he had only been conscious of a kind of ecstatic bliss in the society of other Yogīs and saints, and was quite ready to be buried over again.

What amount of fraud, if any, there may be in these feats it is impossible to say. The phenomena may possibly be accounted for by the fact that Indian Yogīs have studied the habits of hibernating animals for ages.

I may add that it is commonly believed throughout India that a man whose body is sublimated by intense abstract meditation never dies, in the sense of undergoing corruption and dissolution. When his supposed death occurs he is held to be in a state of trance, which may last for centuries, and his body is, therefore, not burnt, but buried—generally in a sitting posture—and his tomb is called a samādh.

With regard to the fifth requisite—the act of withdrawing the senses from their object, as, for example, the eye from visible forms—this is well compared to the act of a tortoise withdrawing its limbs under its shell.

The sixth requisite—fixing the principle of thought—comprises the act of directing the thinking faculty (citta) towards various parts of the body, for example, towards the heart, or towards the crown of the head, or concentrating the will-force on the region between the two eyebrows, or even fixing the eyes intently on the tip of the nose. (Compare *Bhagavad-gītā*, vi. 13.)

The seventh and eighth requisites—viz., internal self-contemplation and intense self-concentration—are held (when conjoined with the sixth) to be most important as leading to the acquisition of certain supernatural powers, of which the following are most commonly enumerated :—(1) Animan, "the faculty of reducing the body to the size of an atom"; (2) Mahiman, or Gariman, "increasing the size or weight at will"; (3) Laghiman, "making the body light at will"; (4) Prāpti, "reaching or touching any object or spot, however apparently distant"; (5) Prākāmya, "unlimited exercise of will"; (6) Isitva, "gaining absolute power over one's self and others"; (7) Vasitā, "bringing the elements into subjection"; (8) Kāmāvasāyitā, "the power of suppressing all desires."

A Yogī who has acquired these powers can rise aloft to the skies, fly through space, pierce the mysteries of planets and stars, cause storms and earthquakes, understand the language of animals, ascertain what occurs in any part of the world, or of the universe, recollect the events of his own previous lives, prolong his present life, see into the past and future, discern the thoughts of others, assume any form he likes, disappear, reappear, and even enter into another man's body and make it his own.

Such were some of the extravagant ideas which grew with the growth of the Yoga system, and all these exist in the later developments of Buddhism. The Buddha himself is fabled by his followers to have ascended to the Trayas-trinsa heaven of Indra, walked on water, stepped from one mountain to another, and left impressions of his feet on the solid rock; although in the well-known *Dhamma-pada* it is twice declared (254, 255), "There is no path through the air."

Of course it was only natural that, with the development of Buddhism and its association with Saivism, the Buddha himself should have become a centre for the growth and accumulation of supernatural and mystical ideas. It is in this way that the later doctrine makes every Buddha have a threefold existence or possess three bodies, much in the same way as in Hindūism three bodies are assigned to every being.

The first of the Buddha's bodies is the Dharma-kāya "body of the Law," supposed to be a kind of ethereal essence of a highly sublimated nature and co-extensive with space. This essence was believed to be eternal, and after the Buddha's death, was represented by the Law or Doctrine (Dharma) he taught. Its Brāhmanical analogue is probably Brahman, "the Universal Spirit," which, when associated with Illusion (or the Kārana-sarīra), may assume a highly ethereal subtle body, called Linga-sarīra.

The second body is the Sambhoga-kāya, "body of conscious bliss," which is of a less ethereal and more material nature than the last. Its Brāhmanical analogue appears to be the intermediate celestial body belonging to departed spirits, called Bhoga-deha, which is of an ethereal character, though it is composed of sufficiently gross (sthūla) material particles to be capable of experiencing happiness in heaven.

The third body is the Nirmāna-kāya, "body of visible shapes and transformations," that is to say, those visible concrete material forms in which every Buddha who exists as an invisible and eternal essence, is manifested on the earth or elsewhere for the propagation of the true doctrine. The Brāhmanical analogue of this third body appears to be the earthly gross body, called Sthūla-sarīra.

There is a well-known legend which relates how the great Brāhman sage Sankarācārya entranced his gross body, and then, having forced out his soul along with his subtle body, entered the dead body of a recently deceased King, which he occupied for several weeks.

In connexion with these mystical ideas, I may here allude to the belief that certain modern Eastern sages, skilled in occult science, have the power of throwing their gross bodies into a state of mesmeric trance, and then by a determined effort of will projecting or forcing out the ethereal body through the pores of the skin, and making this phantasmal form visible in distant places.*

We learn from Mr. Sinnett that a community of Buddhist "Brothers" called Mahātmas, are now living in secluded spots in the deserts of Tibet, who have emancipated their interior selves from physical bondage by meditation, and are believed to possess "astral" or ethereal bodies (distinct from their gross bodies), with which they are able to rise in the air, or move through space, by the mere exercise of will.

I am not aware whether the Psychical Research Society has extended its researches to the deserts of Tibet, where these phenomena are said to take place.

In curious agreement with these notions, are the beliefs of various uncivilised races. Dr. Tylor, in his *Primitive Culture* (I. 440), relates how the North American Indians and others believe that their souls quit their bodies during sleep, and go about hunting, dancing, visiting, etc.

Old legends relate how Simon Magus made statues walk; how he flew in the air; changed his shape; assumed two faces; made the vessels in a house seem to move of themselves (Yule's *Marco Polo*, i. 306). Friar Ricold relates that "a man from India was said to fly. The truth was that he

---

* Colonel Olcott and Mr. Sinnett mention this faculty as characteristic of Asiatic occultism.

did walk close to the surface of the ground without touching it" (Yule's *Marco Polo*, i. 307).

As to the phenomena of modern spiritualism, these are declared by Mr. Sinnett to be quite distinct from those of Asiatic occultism. He maintains that modern spiritualism requires the intervention of " mediums," who neither control nor understand the manifestations of which they are the passive instruments; whereas the phenomena of occultism are the " achievements of a conscious living operator," produced by a simple effort of his own will. The important point, he adds, " which occultism brings out is, that the soul of man, while something enormously subtler and more ethereal and more lasting than the body, is itself a material body. . . . . The ether that transmits light is held to be material by any one who holds it to exist at all; but there is a gulf of difference between it and the thinnest of the gases." In another place he advances an opinion that the spirit is distinct from the soul. It is the soul of the soul.

And again: "The body is the prison of the soul for ordinary mortals. We can see merely what comes before its windows; we can take cognisance only of what is brought within its bars. But the adept has found the key of his prison, and can emerge from it at pleasure. It is no longer a prison for him—merely a dwelling. In other words, the adept can project his soul out of his body to any place he pleases with the rapidity of thought."*

It is worth noting that many believers in Asiatic occultism hold that a hitherto unsuspected force exists in nature called Odic force (is this to be connected with Psychic force?), and that it is by this that the levitation of entranced persons is effected. Some are said to have the power of lightening their bodies by swallowing large draughts of air. The President of the Theosophical Society, Colonel Olcott, alleges that he himself, in common with many other observers, has seen a person raised in the air by a mere effort of will.

Surely these phenomena may be mere feats of conjuring. In the *Asiatic Monthly Journal* for March, 1829, an account is given of a Brāhman who poised himself *apparently* in the air, about four feet from the ground, for forty minutes, in the presence of the Governor of Madras. Another juggler sat on three sticks put together to form a tripod. These were removed, one by one, and the man remained sitting in the

---

* *The Occult World*, by A. P. Sinnett, Vice-President of the Theosophical Society, pp. 12, 15, 20.

air. On the other hand, it is contended, that "since we have attained, in the last half-century, the theory of evolution, the antiquity of man, the far greater antiquity of the world itself, the correlation of physical forces, the conservation of energy, spectrum analysis, photography, the locomotive engine, electric telegraph, spectroscope, electric light, and the telephone, who shall dare to fix a limit to the capacity of man?"* Few will be disposed to deny altogether the truth of such a contention, however much they may dissent from Colonel Olcott's theosophical and neo-Buddhist views.

There may be, of course, latent faculties in humanity which are at present quite unsuspected, and yet are capable of development in the future.

I may also refer to the statement of Sir James Paget, in his recent address on "Scientific Study," that many things now held to be inconceivable and past man's imagination are profoundly and assuredly true, and that it will be in the power of Science to prove them to be so.†

Clearly mystical Buddhism is far too big a subject to be compressed within the limits of a single paper.

I will merely, in conclusion, express my doubts whether Asiatic occultism, as connected with the Yoga philosophy, and as believed in by Colonel Olcott, Mr. Sinnett, and many others, will ever bear the searching light of European scientific investigation.

Nevertheless, it seems to me to be a subject which ought not to be brushed aside by our scientists as unworthy of consideration. It furnishes, in my opinion, a highly interesting topic of inquiry, especially in its bearing on the so-called "Spiritualism," "neo-Buddhism," and "Theosophy" of the present day. The practices connected with mesmerism, animal magnetism, clairvoyance, thought-reading, &c., have their counterparts in the Yoga system prevalent in India more than 2,000 years ago. "The thing that hath been, it is that which shall be; and that which is done is that which shall be done: and there is no new thing under the sun."

---

* Colonel Olcott's *Lectures on Theosophy and Archaic Religions*, p. 109.
† Report in the *Times* newspaper.

www.ingramcontent.com/pod-product-compliance
Lightning Source LLC
Chambersburg PA
CBHW022129090426
42743CB00008B/1073